D1568405

Faatimah
&
Ahmed

This book belongs to

_____

and I'm a Little Muslim

We're Little Muslims

Written By Razeena Gutta

Illustrated By Abira Das

"Assalaamu Alaikum my name is Faatimah, and this is my brother Ahmed."

"We're little Muslims!"

"I am four years old and I love rainbows! I am learning to ride a bicycle but I keep falling off. Luckily, Ahmed teaches me how to ride and helps me up when I fall down. I also love to play hopscotch and have tea parties with my teddies. I am still learning my ABC's and ا ب ت. My brother is very good at ABC's. He is six years old!"

"He loves kites and paper planes. He is very good at flying them, but I'm not. Ahmed also likes to play soccer with his friends and he likes to help mum cook. His favourite food is spaghetti! Spaghetti is so messy. When I try to eat it, it goes all over my face."

"Today was Ahmed's first day at school. I really missed him. When I turn six I will go to school with him. I can't wait! I will learn about numbers and letters and shapes.

I will also learn about drawing and writing. My favourite part of school will be listening to stories. I love stories!"

"I think I'll ask him to tell me a story when he comes home.

Look, here he comes!"

"Faatimah," shouts Ahmed,

"School was such fun! We drew and looked at

shapes and I even played soccer with my friends.

Did you have a good day?"

"Yes Ahmed," said Faatimah. "But tell me, tell me, what did you learn today? Can you tell me a story?"

"Our teacher told us about our Prophet Muhammad (SAW). Let's go inside and I'll tell you all about him."

"He was born a very long time ago. He was sent by Allah to teach the world about Islam. His mother's name was Aaminah. His father's name was Abdullah and his grandfather's name was Abdul Muttalib."

"He was born in Makkah, Faatimah. That's over here. It's a desert, in Arabia."

Wow. A desert, thought Faatimah.

A desert is a hot, sandy place. There aren't many trees there, but it is still very beautiful.

Camels live in the desert.

Faatimah loves camels. They are so different from any other animal.

They are large and brown and they have humps on their backs. Camels can walk on the hot sand, without sinking into it.

They can also store food in their tummies and eat it whenever they need to. That is quite clever of them!

To stand up, camels first raise their back legs, and then their front legs, and this makes the person riding the camel feel very wobbly. Faatimah thought this was really funny!

She loved to daydream and was imagining herself and Ahmed riding on a camel. They were having such fun!

"Are you listening Faatimah?
Stop daydreaming!
There was something amazing
about the night that
Muhammad (SAW) was born.
There was a very bright light that
shone far into the distance.

This was a sign that something important had happened. It was a miracle! We are so lucky that Allah sent him down for us, so that we can learn to be good Muslims."

"Tell me more Ahmed! I want to know more about Muhammad (SAW).

Mom says I was born on a Monday in Safar. When was he born?"

month

yea

Muharram
Safar
Rabbiul-Awwal
Rabi-Uthani
Jumadiul-Awwal
Jumadi-Uthani
Rajab
Sha'ban
Ramadan
Shawwal
Dhul-Qa'da
Dhul-Hijja

"It was the year 570. He was also born on a Monday, but in the month of Rabbiul-Awwal."

week

Monday
Tuesday
Wednesday
Thursday
Friday
Saturday
Sunday

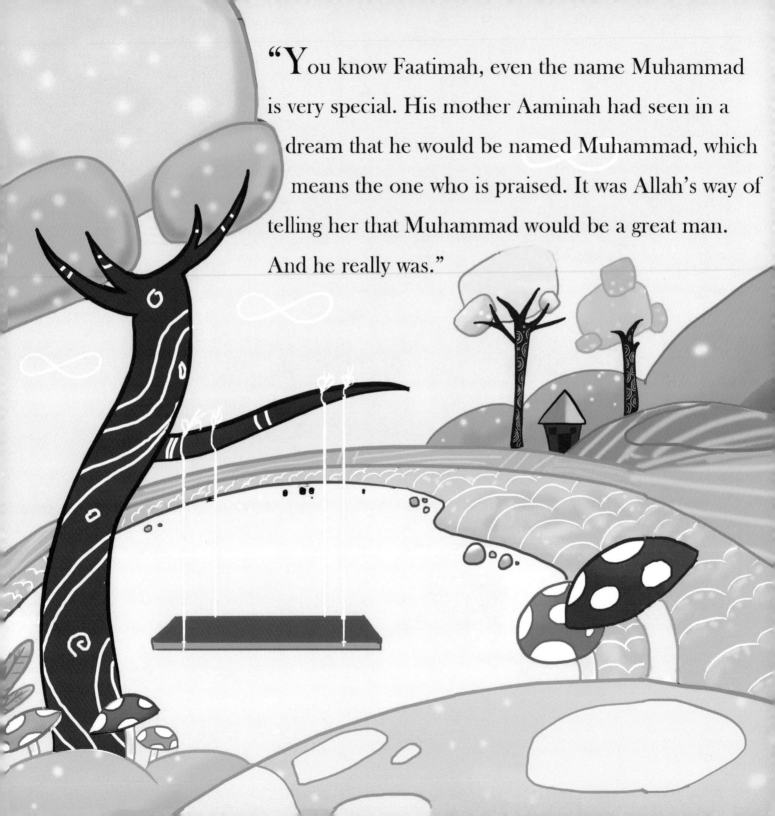

"You know Faatimah, even the name Muhammad is very special. His mother Aaminah had seen in a dream that he would be named Muhammad, which means the one who is praised. It was Allah's way of telling her that Muhammad would be a great man. And he really was."

"He was always truthful, kind and helpful. He loved children and always looked after people who needed help."

"He taught Islam to the people of Arabia and after that, Islam spread all over the world. He is so important to us. We even say a special du'a for him and his family in every Salaah."

"I am going to try my best to be like Muhammad (SAW). I will learn all about him and then I can tell you more, ok?"

"Good idea Ahmed," replied Faatimah, sleepily.

"We will learn all about Muhammad (SAW) so we can be great Muslims too!"

Glossary

ا ب ت - The first three letters of the Arabic alphabet Alif, Baa, Taa

Allah - The Arabic word for God

Assalaamu Alaikum - Muslim greeting meaning May peace be upon you

Du'a - To ask Allah for something

Islam - The religion whose followers believe that there is only one God (Allah) and that Muhammad was the last and final prophet sent to mankind by Allah

Muslim - Someone who follows the religion of Islam

SAW - An abbreviation for the words sallallahu alayhi wasalam, which mean May Allah's peace and blessings be upon him. Muslims say this after referring to the Prophet Muhammad, as a sign of respect and love for him

Salaah - The prayer of a Muslim.

AssalaamuAlaikum.
The aim of the book, *Faatimah and Ahmed: We're little Muslims*, is to be the first resource that can be used to introduce children, as young as two or three, to who Muhammad (SAW) is.

The book is intended for children from the age of 2-6.

The following guide illustrates how the book can be adapted for the different ages.

Ages 2 and 3
Reading to children of this age is very important for their early development. It helps develop their social skills, build their vocabulary and most importantly it is an enjoyable experience for both parent and toddler; even by just flicking through the pages, looking at pictures and picking out the details which interest the child. Whilst they may not concentrate for the entire story, or understand the deeper details, use this book to introduce them to the characters Faatimah and Ahmed, highlighting the fact that they are little Muslims, they believe in Allah and the Prophet Muhammad (SAW) and that they love to pray and learn. As they get older, they will understand more about the concepts and be able to relate to the characters when, for example, they pray alongside their parents or learn about Allah in different ways.

Ages 4 and 5
Children this age start having a deeper curiosity about being Muslim. They may start asking questions about Salaah or Allah, and this book can then be used to explain to them, with the help of Ahmed and Faatimah, the very basics of belief in one God, that Muhammad (SAW) was the final prophet, sent to teach us about Islam. I would encourage you to elaborate as much as the child is curious. They may even be ready to memorise the names of the Prophet's (SAW) parents and grandfather, and where and when he was born. Using fun, engaging characters like Faatimah and Ahmed, that children can relate to, will make it easier to explain what it means to be Muslim.

Ages 6 and up
Most children of this age have already been introduced to the Prophet Muhammad (SAW) by either their parents or teachers. This book will make it fun to learn more about him. The eagerness that Faatimah and Ahmed show toward learning more about Muhammad (SAW) will encourage children of this age to do the same. Additionally, they will now be able to remember the details of the Prophet's (SAW) parents, where and when he was born and perhaps even learn the months of the Islamic calendar. Again, I would encourage parents and teachers to elaborate as much as the child is curious.

The following sources were used when compiling this book –
Sheikh Abdul Nasir Jangda's Seerah series podcasts, available on http://www.qalaminstitute.org, *Muhammad: His Life Based on the Earliest Sources* by Martin Lings and *In the Footsteps of the Prophet* by Tariq Ramadan

I would encourage parents and teachers to refer to these sources for more specific information.

Copyright © 2015 words and illustrations Razeena Gutta

ISBN: 978-1-925209-12-9
Published by Vivid Publishing
P.O. Box 948, Fremantle
Western Australia 6959
www.vividpublishing.com.au

Cataloguing-in-Publication data is available from the National Library of Australia.